MANNERS FOR LIFE

BY: RIGA M.D.

Published and written by Riga M.D.

ISBN: 978-1-7347827-0-7

Copyright © 2020 Riga M.D.

Printed in the U.S.A

riga786@comcast.net

Dear Parents/Caregivers:

Having good manners is an incredibly important life skill. Parents/caregivers are role models for their children. After all, children DO what they SEE.

My father often uses a symbolic relationship between children and plants. He says that, "children are like saplings", they often grow and mold based on how you plant the seedling and provide essential elements such as sunlight, water, air and nutrients. Though a seedling relies on their roots to guide them, children rely on their parents/caregivers to provide them a nurturing environment for growth.

This book is dedicated to parents and caregivers who want to empower their child with good manners. I encourage parents/caregivers to use the book, **"MANNERS FOR LIFE"** as part of their daily interaction with children to solidify the foundation of manners and etiquettes to better prepare them for their lives ahead. Ultimately, our children are our future. Children and saplings require a solid foundation for their roots to grow, and this book is where it all begins!

Hi! I am Noah.

Let's learn our manners! 😊

Saying "Thank you"

I said thank you to my mom when she taught me how to tie my shoelaces.

When I say thank you, I appreciate what my mom has done for me!

I helped my grandpa find his missing glasses. I received a kiss from him once I found it.

I am kind and gentle to my elders!

Helping Others

When my dad is washing the car in the driveway, I make sure I use my manners by helping him wash the car.

Helping others makes me happy!

When I accidently dropped and broke my cereal bowl, I apologized and offered my mom to help clean up.

When I apologize, I am taking responsibility for my actions!

Sharing is Caring

I share my toys whenever my friends come over.
We put them away when we are done playing.

Everyone gets to play when I share!

Being Gentle and Kind

I am kind to everyone, even pets. I try not to squeeze them too hard.

I am always kind and show that I care!

Cleaning up After Yourself

I clean my room and put my toys away, even my kitty cleans after himself.

Cleaning is a great habit!

Always knock

My mom says it is polite and good manners that I knock on the door before I enter someone's room, or home.

Knocking is respecting other's privacy!

Covering your mouth

When I eat, I take small bites and chew with my mouth closed. I get a high five from my mom after every meal.

Eating with your mouth closed is a good table manner!

Smiling

My uncle smiles every time he sees me. I like his big smile a lot! I need to teach my kitty how to smile.

Smiling makes me very happy!

THE END

Making Manners Fun!

Use the following pages to practice a few good manners with your child. Help your child be creative and draw his/her own illustration.

<u>Illustration Page</u>

Illustration Page

Illustration Page

www.ingramcontent.com/pod-product-compliance
Lightning Source LLC
Chambersburg PA
CBHW042104040426
42448CB00002B/141